POM✻POM KITTIES

Make Your Own Cute Cats

BY THE EDITORS OF KLUTZ

KLUTZ®

MEOW!

CONTENTS

You can follow the step-by-step
directions to make the specific
cats in this book, but don't feel
limited by them. Once you get the
hang of making pom-pom kitties,
it's easy to adjust the colors, patterns, tails,
and trim to make any kind of kitty you want.

4 COLORS
OF YARN

BLACK

WHITE

GRAY

ORANGE

What YOU GET

EYES

POM-POM
CHEEKS

POM-POM
CHINS

POM-POM
NOSES

POM-POM MAKER
(4 PIECES)

PIPE CLEANERS

STYLING COMB

GLUE

GLUE
.17oz/5ml

PUNCH-OUT EARS, COLLARS & MORE

WHAT YOU NEED

- Fingernail clippers
- Scissors (ones with thin blades like these work best)

GETTING STARTED

YARN CHARTS

To make the proper pom-poms for each kitty, just follow the charts. Every pom-pom will need 8 yards of yarn but the colors will vary. The charts show exactly how much of each color to use and where to wrap them on your pom-pom maker.

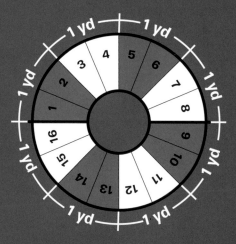

EACH NUMBERED SECTION EQUALS ½ YARD (18 INCHES).

Of course, kitties come in many different colors and patterns. If you want to swap out some of the chart colors for colors of your own choosing, go right ahead.

MEASURING YARN

Use the ruler on the back of this book to measure yarn. Don't pull the yarn so tight that it stretches, or you may not have enough yarn for your pom-pom.

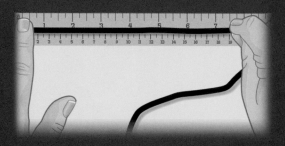

SHORTCUT:

If you wrap your yarn once all the way around the height of the book, that's ½ yard of yarn.

1 YARD		
EQUALS		
1 FOOT	+ 1 FOOT +	1 FOOT
EQUALS		
ABOUT 1 METER		

CUTTING A PIPE CLEANER

- Use fingernail clippers to cut the little bent ends off of each wire.

- Once the ends are clipped, bend the pipe cleaner in half and cut it in the center to make two short pieces.

- You'll need at least half of a pipe cleaner for each of the projects in the book.

TIPS

- Cat grooming can be messy. For easy cleanup, trim your kitty over a container with raised edges, like a cookie sheet, to catch all the little yarn clippings.

- Stash the clippings in a storage baggie for later use. They come in handy when making spots and fluffy puffs.

- These kitties make great gifts for anyone over 6 years old. Do not give finished pom-pom kitties to small children.

- Keep your yarn away from places your pets might try to eat it. Yarn is for pom-pom pets only!

- A solid-colored kitty will use up all of one color of yarn, so look through the whole book before you decide if a solid-colored cat is what you want.

- When you're ready to make more kitties, get additional supplies at your local craft store. Look for yarn labeled "super bulky."

READY?

Start by making a short-haired kitty (page 14). It's the best way to learn the pom-pom kitty basics.

MOM SAYS YOU CAN ONLY TAKE 3 HOME!

FREE KITTENS

THIS BOOK COMES WITH ENOUGH SUPPLIES TO MAKE A LITTER OF 3 KITTIES. LOOK THROUGH THE PAGES OF THE BOOK AND PICK YOUR FAVORITES TO MAKE FIRST.

YOU'LL NEED:

3 PIECES OF YARN
- 2 pieces, 4 yards (4 m) each
- 1 piece, ½ yard (0.5 m)

THE POM-POM MAKER
SCISSORS

MAKING POM·POMS

Each kitty needs two pom-poms—
one for the head and one for the body.
The colors, patterns, and furriness
may change, but the basic pom-pom
is always the same.

1 The pom-pom maker comes in four sections—two with bumps and two with holes. Line up one of the bumpy sections with one of the holey sections, with the bent feet facing out.

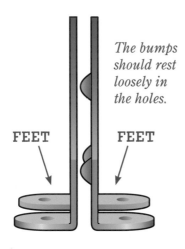

The bumps should rest loosely in the holes.

FEET   FEET

2 Holding the sections together, press the end of a 4-yard (4 m) piece of yarn against the center of the arch.

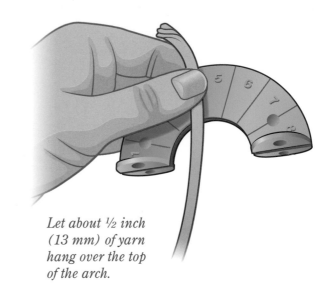

Let about ½ inch (13 mm) of yarn hang over the top of the arch.

3 Wrap the yarn around the pom-pom maker once, crossing over the tail . . .

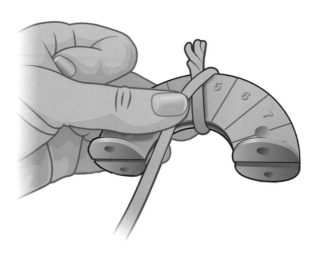

. . . then wrap it around again, crossing over the tail in an X pattern to secure it.

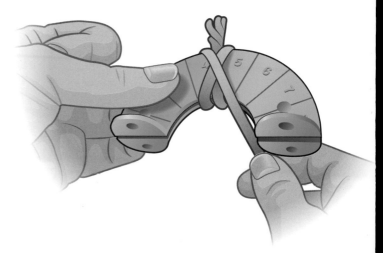

4 Now wrap the yarn around the arch in fairly even rows. Once you reach the end, start wrapping in the other direction, overlapping the wraps you just made.

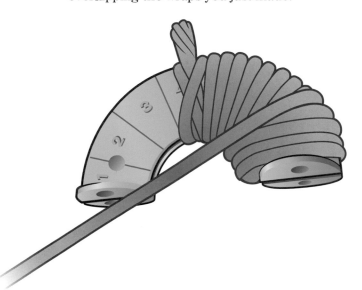

5 Continue wrapping until the entire arch is covered fairly evenly and all the yarn is wrapped.

Wrap right over the tail to hide it.

6 Tuck the loose end securely under some of the wrapped yarn.

If you can't lift the yarn with your fingers, try using the handle of your comb.

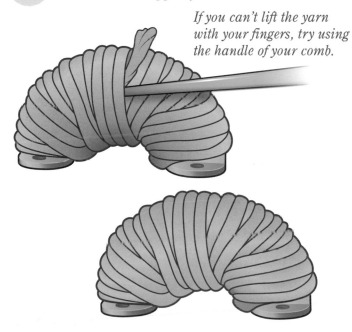

MULTICOLORED POM-POMS

Every color change on the chart is made by wrapping a separate piece of yarn. Start each color of yarn in the center of its section, and wrap as usual.

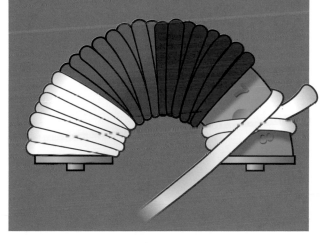

7 Repeat Steps 1–6 with the other 4-yard length of yarn on the other half of the pom-pom maker.

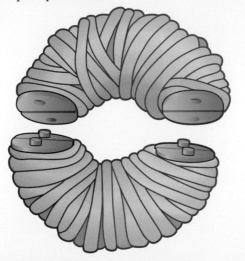

8 Snap the feet of the wrapped arches together.

Make sure all four feet are securely attached.

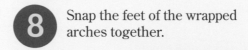 **STOP!** Are you making a body pom-pom?

IF SO, THEN DO THIS EXTRA STEP BEFORE YOU MOVE ON TO STEP 9.

BODY POM-POMS

IT'S IMPORTANT TO ADD YOUR KITTY'S FRONT PAWS AND TAIL NOW. THIS WAY THEY WILL BE SECURED IN THE CENTER OF YOUR FINISHED BODY POM-POM.

- Check the chart to see what color pipe cleaner your cat needs.

- Fold the short pieces (page 5) in half and slide them through the center of the wrapped arches. Pinch the pipe cleaners close to the yarn so they stay in place.

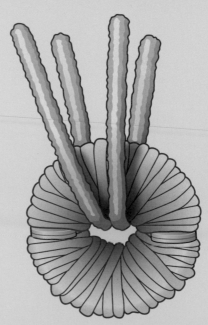

WHAT ARE THE PIPE CLEANERS USED FOR?

Two pieces will become the front legs. One piece will be the tail. The last piece will be hidden inside the pom. A finished kitty sits on its back legs, which are trimmed from the pom-pom yarn.

9 Find the groove between one set of feet in your pom-pom maker and insert one blade of your scissors as far as it will go.

Don't push the blade down toward the center of the pom-pom maker. Run it along the groove around the edge instead.

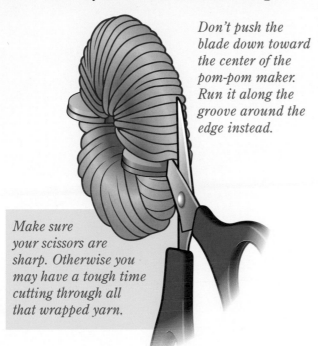

Make sure your scissors are sharp. Otherwise you may have a tough time cutting through all that wrapped yarn.

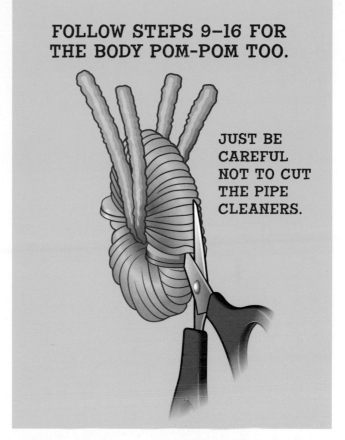

FOLLOW STEPS 9–16 FOR THE BODY POM-POM TOO.

JUST BE CAREFUL NOT TO CUT THE PIPE CLEANERS.

10 Cut along the groove around the entire circle.

As you cut, the yarn pieces will fill in the center of the pom-pom maker.

To make sure the cut pieces stay in the center, keep the pom-pom maker snapped together and don't tug on any of the cut pieces.

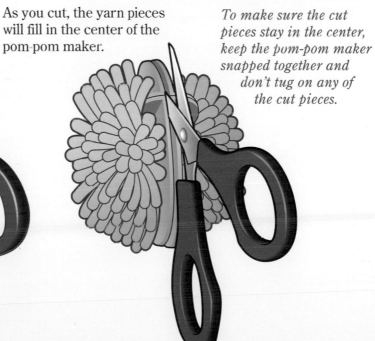

11 Rest the pom-pom maker on a flat surface. Wedge the loose ½-yard (0.5 m) strand of yarn into the groove around the edge of the pom-pom maker, and pull it snug.

It can be tricky to get the yarn into the groove, but you can do it.

12 Tie the strand in a knot, pulling the ends firmly so the knot slides down into the groove and holds the center of the pom-pom together.

TIE IT TIGHT!

13 Pull the ends of the strand to the opposite side of the groove and tie another tight knot there.

It's important to pull the knots tight so your pom-poms will stay together when it's time to transform them into kitties.

14 Tie one more knot in the same spot, just to be sure.

15 Remove the pom-pom maker by popping the pieces apart.

MULTICOLORED POM-POMS

When you tie the center of the pom-pom together, make sure the final knot is in a section with the same color yarn.

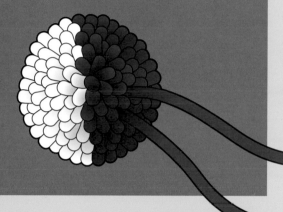

16 Trim the long tails of yarn to the same length as the rest of the pom-pom. Set them aside for now—you will use these scrap pieces later when making kitties.

PURRRRFECT! YOU DID IT!

BE CAREFUL NOT TO CUT THE PIPE CLEANERS ON THE BODY POM-POM.

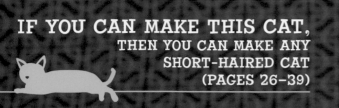
SHORT-HAIRED

Start a longtime friendship with a short-haired cat.

YOU'LL NEED:

- 1 head pom-pom (see chart)
- 1 body pom-pom (see chart)
- 1 pair of eyes
- 1 pink nose pom-pom
- 2 white cheek pom-poms
- 1 white chin pom-pom
- 1 pair of punch-out gray ears
- 1 gray punch-out circle
- Styling comb

YOU CAN MAKE ANY
COLOR CAT YOU WANT,
WE JUST SHOW A GRAY
KITTY AS AN EXAMPLE.

HEAD POM-POM

3 PIECES OF YARN

- 2 gray, 4 yards (4 m) each
- 1 gray to tie the middle, ½ yard (0.5 m)

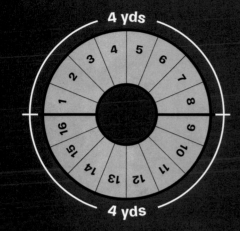

BODY POM-POM

3 PIECES OF YARN

- 2 gray, 4 yards (4 m) each
- 1 gray to tie the middle, ½ yard (0.5 m)

2 PIPE CLEANER PIECES

- 2 gray, 6 inches (15 cm) each

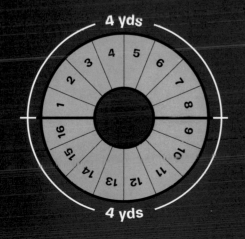

MAKE A HEAD

1 On one of the pom-poms, pinch a tuft of about 6 strands of yarn.

2 Tie the scrap of yarn around the tuft.

See pages 7–13 for pom-pom instructions.

3 Grab the tuft like a handle and trim the rest of the yarn short. Keep trimming until all the strands are about the same length, forming a nice, round ball.

Don't be shy about cutting the yarn short—remember, this will be a short-haired cat. As long as you trim the ball evenly all the way around, it'll look great.

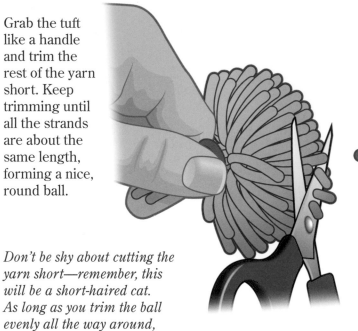

DON'T CUT THIS!

4 Untie the tuft and part it into two equal sections.

5 Pinch one side of the tuft at the base, as close to the center of the ball as you can. (Pinching the yarn keeps it from being pulled out by the comb.) Comb the section to make it fluffy.

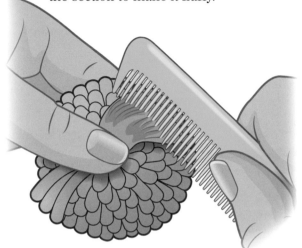

Comb out the other side of the tuft.

THESE ARE THE KITTY'S WHISKERS.

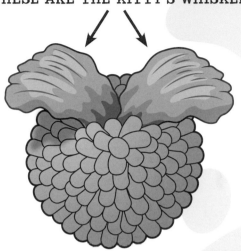

6 Looking directly down at the fluffy whiskers, dab glue near the top of the part.

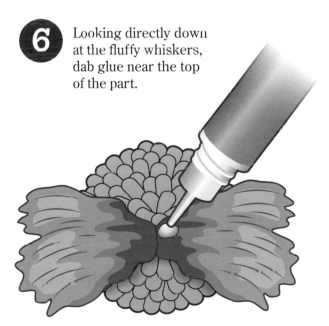

Place a cheek pom-pom in the glue. Wait a minute for it to dry before moving on.

7 Repeat step 6 on the other side of the part. Wait a minute for it to dry before moving on.

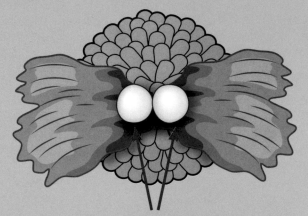

THESE ARE THE KITTY'S CHEEKS.

8 Glue a chin pom-pom under the pom-pom cheeks. Tuck it under the cheeks a little bit. Let the glue dry before moving on.

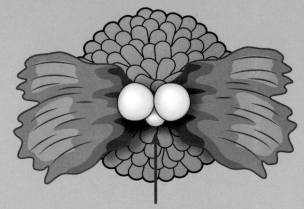

THIS IS THE KITTY'S CHIN.

9 Glue a tiny pink nose pom-pom on top of the pom-pom cheeks. Let the glue dry before moving on.

10 Rotate the pom-pom so the whiskers are facing you. Trim the kitty's whiskers at an angle—shorter at the bottom, longer at the top.

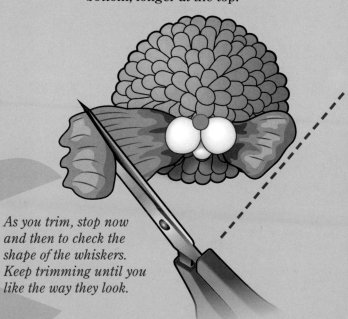

As you trim, stop now and then to check the shape of the whiskers. Keep trimming until you like the way they look.

11 Use your fingertip to make two dents in the pom-pom where you want the eyes to go. Put a dot of glue in each dent, then stick the eyes in place.

Make sure the black parts of the cat's eyes are pointed straight up and down.

THE LOWER AND WIDER YOU SET THE EYES, THE MORE IT WILL LOOK LIKE A BABY KITTEN. Use the outside edge of the cheeks as a guide.

12 Glue the ears in place.

Take a look at your kitty's head and trim any fur that seems out of place.

PUT THE HEAD ASIDE. IT'S TIME TO MOVE ON TO THE BODY.

ATTACHING EARS

BECAUSE KITTIES ARE SO FLUFFY, IT CAN BE TRICKY TO GLUE ON EARS SO THEY STAY PUT.

It's easiest if you use your fingertip to make a dent in the pom-pom where you want the ear to go, and then put a drop of glue in the dent.

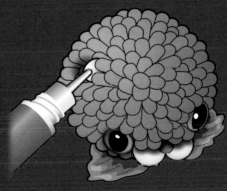

Stick the ear into the glue. Pinch the surrounding yarn against the paper ear and hold it until the glue dries.

MAKE A BODY

REMEMBER, THE PIPE CLEANERS ARE GOING TO BECOME THE FRONT LEGS AND TAIL. CONFUSED? READ ON AND WE'LL SHOW YOU HOW TO MAKE YOUR CAT SIT UP.

1 Slowly tug on one pipe cleaner piece to find its other end. Once you find it, make the pieces even again and separate the two pairs from one another.

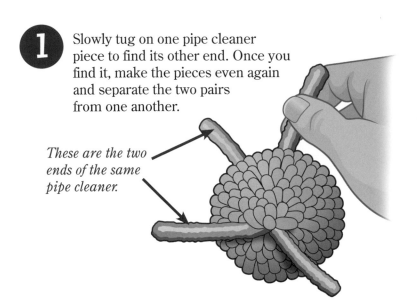

These are the two ends of the same pipe cleaner.

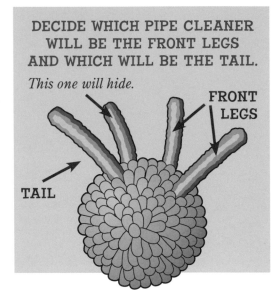

DECIDE WHICH PIPE CLEANER WILL BE THE FRONT LEGS AND WHICH WILL BE THE TAIL.

This one will hide.

FRONT LEGS

TAIL

2 Bend one end of the tail pipe cleaner into a small hook or loop.

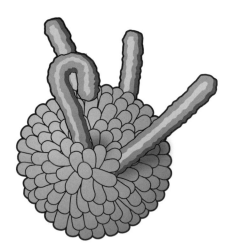

3 Gently pull the unbent end of the tail pipe cleaner until the hook is hidden inside the pom-pom.

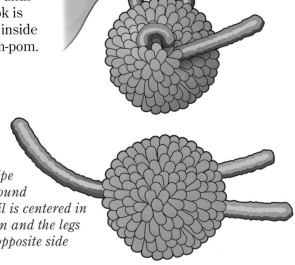

Move the pipe cleaners around until the tail is centered in the pom-pom and the legs are on the opposite side of the body.

4 Tie the scrap yarn around the middle of the body pom-pom. It should be right under the pipe cleaners.

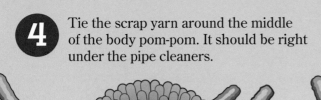

Trim all the yarn on one side of the body pom-pom so it matches the length of the yarn on the head pom-pom you already made. Untie the scrap when you're done trimming.

It doesn't matter which half you trim because you can always adjust the placement of the pipe cleaners later on.

THIS IS THE KITTY'S BELLY.

Leave the yarn on the belly long (for now).

5 Separate the untrimmed half into three equal sections, as shown.

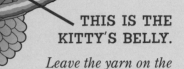

6 Push the two side sections flat and trim just the center section so it matches the trimmed length of the body. You'll end up with two tufts of long yarn separated by a patch of trimmed yarn.

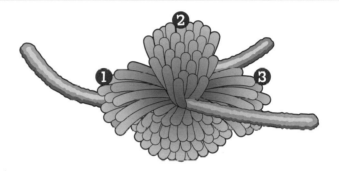

7 Next, trim the long tuft closest to the front leg pipe cleaners. All the yarn by the front legs should be short, so trim anything that looks out of place.

8 Rotate the pom-pom so the front legs are facing you. Divide the remaining tuft into three equal sections and trim the center tuft.

THERE SHOULD BE ONLY THREE STRANDS OF YARN IN EACH TUFT.

If there are more than three strands, then carefully cut off the extra strands until both tufts are even.

THESE ARE THE KITTY'S BACK LEGS.

WATCH OUT! THE CAT'S OUT OF THE BAG.

SUGAR

22

9 Pinch one tuft as close to the center of the ball as you can. Comb out the section to make it fluffy.

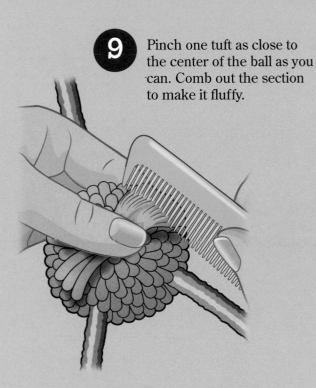

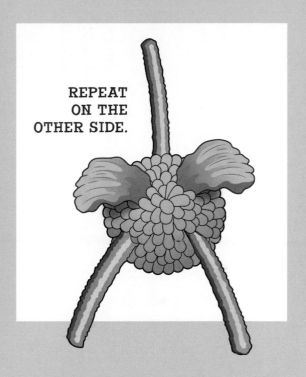

REPEAT ON THE OTHER SIDE.

10 Set the body on its legs. Bend the ends of the front leg pipe cleaners toward the body to make little round paws.

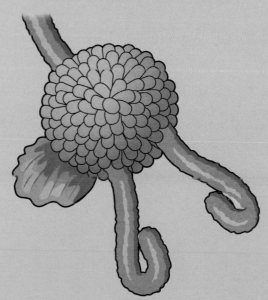

11 Add a little curl at the tip of the tail.

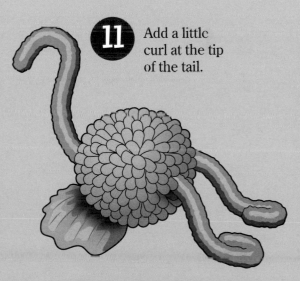

Trim any fur that looks out of place.

ALMOST DONE!

1 Trim the bottom of the head and the top of the body so they are flat.

2 Put a glob of glue on the punch-out circle. Use the tip of the bottle to spread the glue to the edge of the circle.

3 Place the circle, glue side down, in the center of the flat section on top of the body.

4 Add more glue to the top of the circle, spreading it to the edge.

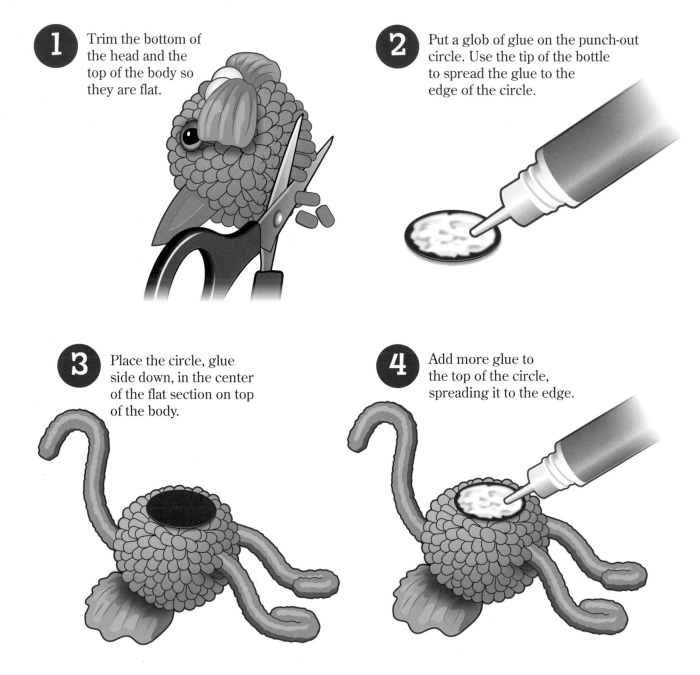

5 Place the head on top of the glued circle.

Center the face above the two pipe cleaner paws.

6 Squish the head and the body together until the glue dries a bit.

Don't worry about hurting your kitty. She'll pop right back up when you're done.

7 Let your cat nap for several minutes, until the glue is completely dry.

YOU GOT IT!

YOUR KITTY COULD BE FINISHED NOW, OR YOU CAN ADD MORE DETAIL WITH SCRAPS OF YARN (PAGE 31).

If your kitty keeps tipping over, make sure to trim her underside nice and flat. You may also need to adjust the paws until she's sitting pretty.

TORTOISESHELL

"Torties" combine great traits together—cute and cuddly.

YOU'LL NEED:

- 1 head pom-pom (see chart)
- 1 body pom-pom (see chart)
- 1 pair of eyes
- 1 pink nose pom-pom
- 2 black cheek pom-poms
- 1 black chin pom-pom
- 1 pair of punch-out black ears
- 1 black punch-out circle
- Styling comb

HEAD POM-POM

5 PIECES OF YARN

- 2 black, 2 yards (2 m) each
- 2 orange, 2 yards (2 m) each
- 1 black to tie the middle, ½ yard (0.5 m)

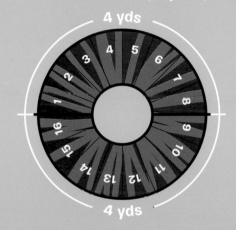

4 yds

4 yds

BODY POM-POM

5 PIECES OF YARN

- 2 black, 2 yards (2 m) each
- 2 orange, 2 yards (2 m) each
- 1 black to tie the middle, ½ yard (0.5 m)

2 PIPE CLEANER PIECES

- 2 black, 6 inches (15 cm) each

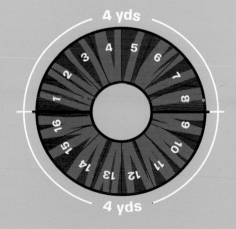

4 yds

4 yds

See pages 7–13 for pom-pom making instructions.

1 Line up the ends of both yarn pieces on the pom-pom maker. You will treat the two strands as if they are one.

2 Wrap the strands together around the arches to make multicolored head and body pom-poms (pages 7–13).

WRAP WITHOUT WORRY!

It's OK if the different colors wrap over each other. It will make your kitty look more speckled.

3 Follow the directions on pages 14–25 to make a short-haired cat.

TRY ME IN DIFFERENT COLORS

CALICO

Make a special spot in your heart for this adorable kitty.

YOU'LL NEED:

- 1 head pom-pom (see chart)
- 1 body pom-pom (see chart)
- 1 pair of eyes
- 1 pink nose pom-pom
- 2 white cheek pom-poms
- 1 white chin pom-pom
- 1 pair of punch-out white ears
- 1 white punch-out circle
- Styling comb

HEAD POM-POM

6 PIECES OF YARN

- 2 white, 1 yard (1 m) each
- 1 orange, 1 yard (1 m)
- 1 black, 1 yard (1 m)
- 1 white, 4 yards (4 m)
- 1 white to tie the middle, ½ yard (0.5 m)

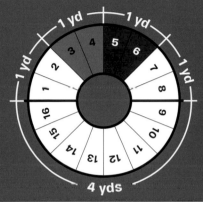

BODY POM-POM

11 PIECES OF YARN

- 4 white, 1 yard (1 m) each
- 1 white, 1 ½ yards (1.5 m)
- 2 orange, ½ yard (0.5 m) each
- 3 black, ½ yard (0.5 m) each
- 1 white to tie the middle, ½ yard (0.5 m)

2 PIPE CLEANER PIECES

- 2 white, 6 inches (15 cm) each

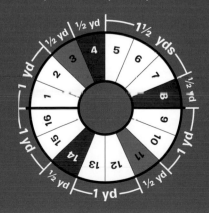

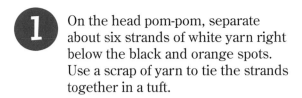

1 On the head pom-pom, separate about six strands of white yarn right below the black and orange spots. Use a scrap of yarn to tie the strands together in a tuft.

2 Grab the tuft like a handle and trim the rest of the yarn short, so it forms a nice, round ball.

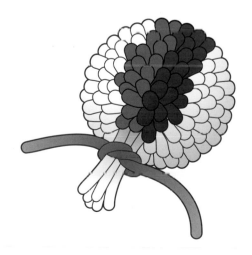

See pages 7–13 for pom-pom making instructions.

3 Untie the tuft and comb it out. Part the fluffed tuft and glue on the cheeks, chin, and nose at the bottom of the black and orange spots (pages 17–18 , Steps 5–10). Trim the whiskers however you like.

4 Glue on the eyes and ears (page 19, Steps 11–12).

5 Make the body pom-pom with pipe cleaners (pages 20–23). Move the yarn around until the spots look good to you.

6 Attach the head to the body (pages 24–25).

 WANNA BE FRIENDS?

YOUR PET IS UNIQUELY YOURS. NO TWO CATS HAVE TO LOOK THE SAME.

ADDING UNIQUE SPOTS & MARKINGS

IT'S EASY TO MAKE A NEW BREED OR THE TWIN TO YOUR CAT AT HOME.

Glue the ends of tiny yarn clippings directly into the fur to make patterns. The handle of the comb can help you push the clippings deep into the pom-poms.

TUXEDO

Meet a classy cat who always dresses to impress.

YOU'LL NEED:

- 1 head pom-pom (see chart)
- 1 body pom-pom (see chart)
- 1 pair of eyes
- 1 pink nose pom-pom
- 2 white cheek pom-poms
- 1 white chin pom-pom
- 1 pair of punch-out black ears
- 1 black punch-out circle
- Styling comb

HEAD POM-POM

5 PIECES OF YARN

- 1 black, 1 ½ yards (1.5 m)
- 1 black, 2 yards (2 m)
- 1 black, 4 yards (4 m)
- 1 white, ½ yard (0.5 m)
- 1 black to tie the middle, ½ yard (0.5 m)

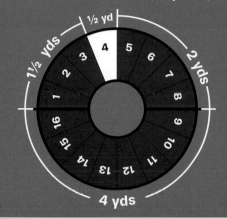

BODY POM-POM

3 PIECES OF YARN

- 1 black, 4 yards (4 m)
- 1 white, 4 yards (4 m)
- 1 black to tie the middle, ½ yard (0.5 m)

2 PIPE CLEANER PIECES

- 2 black, 6 inches (15 cm) each

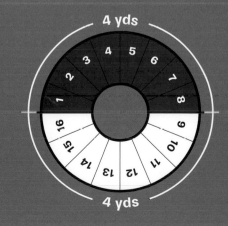

1 On the head pom-pom, separate about six pieces of white yarn. Use a scrap of yarn to tie the six pieces together in a tuft.

2 Grab the tuft like a handle and trim the rest of the yarn short, so it forms a nice, round ball.

THIS IS THE STRIPE ABOVE THE KITTY'S NOSE.

See pages 7–13 for pom-pom making instructions.

3 Untie the tuft and comb it out. Part the fluffed tuft and glue on the cheeks, chin, and nose inside the white stripe (pages 17–18 , Steps 5–10). Trim the whiskers however you like.

4 Glue on the eyes and ears (page 19, Steps 11–12).

5 Make a body pom-pom with pipe cleaners (pages 20–23).

6 Move the yarn ends around so there is some white yarn on the kitty's chest, between the front paws.

7 Attach the head to the body (pages 24–25).

MAKE ME IN **OPPOSITE COLORS**

COOL CATS!

THEY HAVE MITTENS ON!

EXTRA STEPS

KITTEN MITTENS

ADD DIFFERENT-COLORED PAWS TO YOUR CAT.
YOU CAN DO THE SAME THING AT THE TIP OF THE TAIL.

- Cut two 3-inch (8 cm) pieces of pipe cleaner.

- Wrap one around the bottom of one of the front legs, starting at the paw (the loop) and going all the way to the end of the foot.

- Repeat on the other leg.

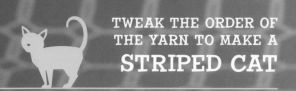
TABBY

Pet a tabby and start your streak of good luck.

YOU'LL NEED:

- 1 head pom-pom (see chart)
- 1 body pom-pom (see chart)
- 1 pair of eyes
- 1 pink nose pom-pom
- 2 white cheek pom-poms
- 1 white chin pom-pom
- 1 pair of punch-out white ears
- 1 white punch-out circle
- Styling comb

HEAD POM-POM

9 PIECES OF YARN

- 4 white, 1 yard (1 m) each
- 4 orange, 1 yard (1 m) each
- 1 white to tie the middle, ½ yard (0.5 m)

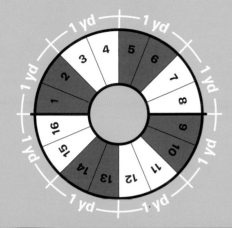

BODY POM-POM

9 PIECES OF YARN

- 4 white, 1 yard (1 m) each
- 4 orange, 1 yard (1 m) each
- 1 white to tie the middle, ½ yard (0.5 m)

2 PIPE CLEANER PIECES

- 2 white, 6 inches (15 cm) each

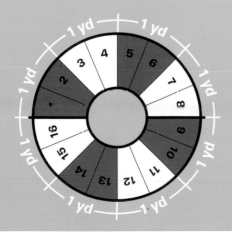

1 On the head pom-pom, separate about six strands of white yarn. Use a scrap of yarn to tie the pieces together in a tuft.

2 Grab the tuft like a handle and trim the rest of the yarn short, so it forms a nice, round ball.

3 Move around the cut ends of the white and orange yarn until they form straight stripes.

See pages 7–13 for pom-pom making instructions.

4 Untie the tuft and comb it out. Part the fluffed tuft and glue the cheeks, chin, and nose inside a white stripe (pages 17–18, Steps 5–10). Trim the whiskers however you like.

5 Glue on the eyes and ears (page 19, Steps 11–12).

6 Make a body pom-pom with pipe cleaners (pages 20–23). Move the yarn around until the stripes look good to you.

CUTE!

7 Attach the head to the body (pages 24–25).

SHORT OR LONG?

IT'S EASY TO MAKE LONG-HAIRED VERSIONS.

Use the charts from the short-haired cats for patterns, but follow the directions for the long-haired cat. See pages 40–50 to learn how to make long-haired cats and Persians.

 JUST CHANGE THE COLORS
TO CREATE A VARIETY OF
LONG-HAIRED CATS.

LONG-HAIRED

The most fabulous, fluffiest feline.

YOU'LL NEED:

- 1 head pom-pom (see chart)
- 1 body pom-pom (see chart)
- 1 pair of eyes
- 1 pink nose pom-pom
- 2 white cheek pom-poms
- 1 white chin pom-pom
- 1 pair of punch-out white ears
- 1 white punch-out circle
- Styling comb

HEAD POM-POM

3 PIECES OF YARN
- 2 white, 4 yards (4 m) each
- 1 white to tie the middle, ½ yard (0.5 m)

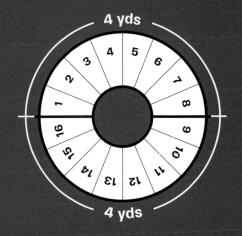

BODY POM-POM

3 PIECES OF YARN
- 2 white, 4 yards (4 m) each
- 1 white to tie the middle, ½ yard (0.5 m)

1 PIECE OF A PIPE CLEANER
- 1 white, 6 inches (15 cm)

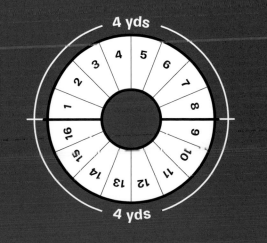

See pages 7–13 for pom-pom making instructions.

MAKE A LONG-HAIRED HEAD

1 Separate a tuft of 20 strands and tie it with a scrap of yarn. Trim the rest of the yarn short to form a nice, round ball (pages 15–16, Steps 1–3).

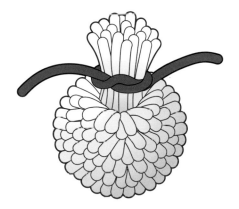

2 With the tuft still tied, pinch a small section of the untied yarn as close to the center of the ball as you can. (Pinching the yarn keeps it from being pulled out by the comb.) Comb the section to make it fluffy.

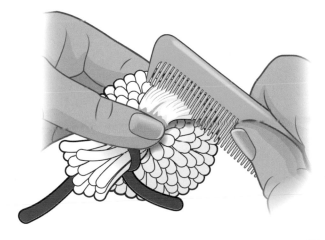

3 Fluff out the rest of the ball the same way, pinching and combing section by section.

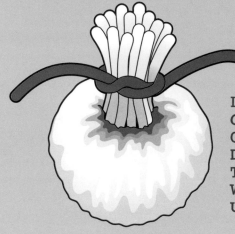

IT'S OKAY IF A COUPLE OF STRANDS OF YARN COME OUT DURING COMBING. THE FLUFFINESS WILL MAKE UP FOR IT.

4 Untie the tuft and part it into two equal sections.

5 Trim the left tuft very close to the pom-pom.

side view

6 Rotate the pom-pom so the patch of short yarn is above the remaining tuft. Separate the tuft into two equal parts.

top view

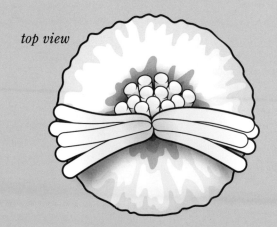

7 Pinch one side of the tuft as close to the center of the ball as you can. Comb out the section to make it fluffy.

Repeat on the other side.

THESE ARE THE KITTY'S WHISKERS.

8 Glue on the cheeks, chin, and nose at the bottom of the patch of short yarn (pages 17–18, Steps 5–10). Trim the whiskers however you like.

9 Glue on the eyes and ears (page 19, Steps 11–12).

PUT THE HEAD ASIDE.
TIME TO MOVE ON
TO THE BODY.

MAKE A LONG-HAIRED BODY

1 When making a long-haired body, add only one pipe cleaner for the front legs. You will make a fluffy yarn tail with scraps (page 45).

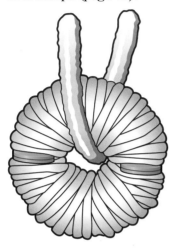

2 Make a body *without* a tail (pages 20–23).

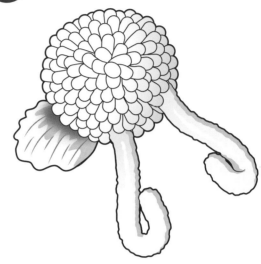

3 Pinch a small section of the yarn as close to the center of the ball as you can. Comb out the section to make it fluffy.

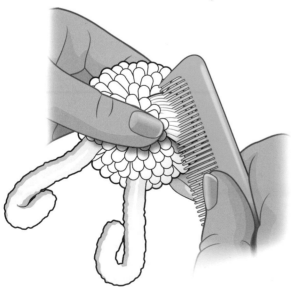

Carefully comb out the entire body.

THE FUR GETS FLUFFIER THE MORE YOU COMB IT.

FLUFFY TAILS

A LONG-HAIRED KITTY NEEDS AN EXTRA FLUFFY TAIL, SO MAKE ONE OUT OF SCRAPS.

• Tie several long scraps of yarn together in the middle. Longer scraps look better.

• Carefully comb the yarn on both sides of the center knot. Fold the whole bundle in the middle and glue the knot directly into the pom-pom.

4 Glue the knot directly into the pom-pom. Use the handle of the comb to help you push in the tail to secure it.

5 Glue the head to the body using a punch-out circle (page 24–25).

6 After the glue is completely dry, give your kitty a final fluff (and a trim, if needed).

PRETTY KITTY!

Use little hair bows from home to accent your cat's fluffy fur.

FLUFFY

PERSIAN

Meet everyone's favorite grumpy cat.

YOU'LL NEED:

- 1 head pom-pom (see chart)
- 1 body pom-pom (see chart)
- 1 pair of eyes
- 1 pink nose pom-pom
- 1 white cheek pom-pom
- 1 pair of punch-out gray ears
- 1 gray punch-out circle
- Styling comb

HEAD POM-POM

3 PIECES OF YARN

- 2 gray, 4 yards (4 m) each
- 1 gray to tie the middle, ½ yard (0.5 m)

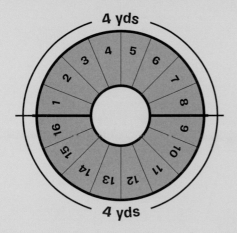

BODY POM-POM

3 PIECES OF YARN

- 2 gray, 4 yards (4 m) each
- 1 gray to tie the middle, ½ yard (0.5 m)

1 PIECE OF A PIPE CLEANER

- 1 white, 6 inches (15 cm)

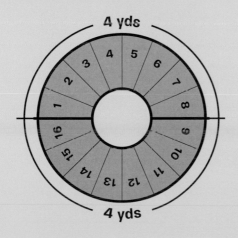

1 Separate a tuft of six strands and tie it with a scrap of yarn. Trim the rest of the yarn short to form a nice, round ball (pages 15–16, Steps 1–3).

2 Fluff out the rest of the ball the same way for a long-haired cat (page 41–42, Steps 2–3), pinching and combing section by section.

See pages 7–13 for pom-pom making instructions.

3 Untie the tuft and part it into three equal sections.

side view

4 Trim the left and right tufts close to the pom-pom, leaving only the middle tuft.

side view

5 Look directly down at the head and separate the remaining tuft into two equal parts. Push one section up and one section down.

top view

6 Trim off the bottom tuft.

7 Pinch the remaining tuft as close to the center of the ball as you can. Comb out the tuft to make it fluffy.

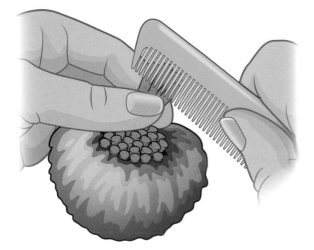

8 Part the fluffed tuft into two equal sections.

THESE ARE THE KITTY'S CHEEKS.

Persians use fur instead of the cheek pom-poms.

9 Glue one cheek pom-pom on to the short yarn, directly under the fluffy whiskers, to make the chin.

Use a bigger (cheek) pom-pom for the chin so that it will show up under all that fur.

top view

10 Rotate the head so the whiskers are facing you. Pull the whiskers down over the pom-pom. Your kitty will look a bit grumpy. Glue a nose on top of the whiskers.

11 Glue on the eyes so they line up with the top of the nose.

To make a perfect Persian face, it's important to never glue the eyes higher then the nose.

12 Finish by adding the ears (page 19).

YOU CAN TRIM THE WHISKERS OR LEAVE THEM LONG, HOWEVER YOU LIKE.

13 Make a long-haired body pom-pom with pipe cleaners and attach a fluffy tail (pages 44–45).

14 Glue the head to the body using a punch-out circle (page 24–25). Wait for the glue to dry, then give your kitty a final grooming.

SOUR-PUSS!

CATTITUDES

DIVA

For your fashionable feline, glue on punch-out collars and tags to customize your cat.

HAPPY

Write your kitty's name or initials on the cat tag.

EXCITED

Ready to play? Raise your cat's front paws up until he looks like he's ready to pounce.

CONTENT

Ready for a cat nap? Glue the head to the front of the body, rather than the top.

MAKE YOUR CAT FEEL AT HOME

Use items from around your house to make mini kitty essentials.

TAKE-OUT CARRIER

RIBBON COLLAR
Attach a little bell from the craft store.

SOCK BED

MINT TIN LITTER BOX

BOTTLE CAP FOOD DISHES

PAPER TUBE SCRATCHING POST